INTRODUCTION

Butterflies and moths belong to the second largest order of insects (next to beetles) with approximately 170,000 species worldwide. All have two pairs of wings covered with overlapping layers of fine scales. They feed by uncoiling a long feeding tube (proboscis) and sucking nutrients from flowers, puddles, etc. When not in use, the tube is coiled under the head.

The two groups differ in several ways:

BUTTERFLIES
- Active by day
- Brightly colored
- Thin body
- Rests with wings held erect over its back
- Antennae are thin and thickened at the tip

MOTHS
- Active at night
- Most are dull-colored
- Stout body
- Rests with wings folded, tent-like, over its back
- Antennae are usually thicker and often feathery

All butterflies and moths have a complex life cycle consisting of four developmental stages.

1. **EGGS** – Eggs are laid singly or in clusters on vegetation or on the ground. One or more clutches of eggs may be laid each year.
2. **CATERPILLARS (LARVAE)** – These worm-like creatures hatch from eggs and feed primarily on plants (often on the host plant on which the eggs were laid). As they grow, larvae shed their skin periodically.
3. **PUPAE** – Pupae are the "cases" within which caterpillars transform into adults. The pupa of a butterfly is known as a chrysalis; those of moths are called cocoons. In cooler regions, pupae often overwinter before maturing into butterflies or moths.
4. **ADULT** – Butterflies/moths emerge from pupae to feed and breed.

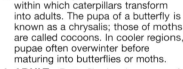

ATTRACTING BUTTERFLIES TO YOUR YARD

1. **Food** – Almost all butterfly caterpillars eat plants; adult butterflies feed almost exclusively on plant nectar. Your local garden shop, library and bookstore will have information on which plants attract specific species.
2. **Water** – Soak the soil in your garden or sandy areas to create puddles. These provide a source of water and minerals.
3. **Rocks** – Put large flat rocks in sunny areas. Butterflies will gather there to spread their wings and warm up.
4. **Brush** – Small brush piles and hollow logs provide ideal places for butterflies to lay their eggs and hibernate over the winter.

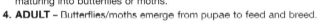

Most illustrations show the upper wings of males unless otherwise noted. The measurements denote the wingspan of species. Note that wing shape differs in flight and at rest. Illustrations are not to scale.

Waterford Press publishes reference guides that introduce readers to nature observation, outdoor recreation and survival skills. Product information is featured on the website: www.waterfordpress.com

978-1-62005-442-0
Made in the USA
$7.95 U.S.
50795
ISBN 9 781620 054420
UPC 8 84682 01401 8
1 0 9 8 7 6 5 4 3 2 1   2210502

ALASKA BUTTERFLIES & POLLINATORS

A Folding Pocket Guide to Familiar Species

SWALLOWTAILS & ALLIES

This family includes the largest butterfly species. Most are colorful and have a tail-like projection on each hindwing.

Old World Swallowtail
Papilio machaon
To 2.5 in. (6 cm)

Canadian Tiger Swallowtail
Papilio canadensis
To 3 in. (8 cm)

Eversmann's Parnassian
Parnassius eversmanni
To 2.25 in. (5.2 cm)
This 'must-see' Arctic species is the only yellow parnassian.

Phoebus Parnassian
Parnassius phoebus
To 3 in. (8 cm)
Red-spotted cream to snow-white butterfly.

WHITES & SULPHURS

White and yellow/orange butterflies are among the first to appear in spring.

Sara Orangetip
Anthocharis sara
To 1.5 in. (4 cm)
Common in meadows in spring and summer.

Great Northern Sulphur
Colias gigantea
To 3 in. (8 cm)

Hecla Sulphur
Colias hecla
To 1.75 in. (4.5 cm)

Labrador Sulphur
Colias nastes
To 1.75 in. (4.5 cm)

WHITES & SULPHURS

Palaeno Sulphur
Colias palaeno
To 1.75 in. (4.5 cm)

Common Sulphur
Colias philodice
To 2 in. (5 cm)
Common in open areas and along roadsides.

Creamy Marblewing
Euchloe ausonides
To 3 in. (8 cm)

Northern Marblewing
Euchloe creusa
To 1.5 in. (4 cm)

Arctic White
Pieris angelika
To 1.5 in. (4 cm)

Veined White
Artogeia napi
To 1.5 in. (4 cm)

Cabbage White
Pieris rapae
To 2 in. (5 cm)
One of the most common butterflies. Feeds on cabbage leaves and wild mustards.

Western White
Pontia occidentalis
To 1.5 in. (4 cm)

SKIPPERS

Named for their fast, bouncing flight, skippers have distinctive antennae that end in curved clubs.

Arctic Skipper
Carterocephalus palaemon
To 1 in. (3 cm)

Perseus Duskywing
Erynnis persius
To 1.5 in. (4 cm)

Common Branded Skipper
Hesperia comma
To 1 in. (3 cm)

Grizzled Skipper
Pyrgus centaureae
To 1.25 in. (3.2 cm)

GOSSAMER-WINGED BUTTERFLIES

This family of small bluish or coppery butterflies often has small, hair-like tails on its hindwings. Most rest with their wings folded and underwings exposed.

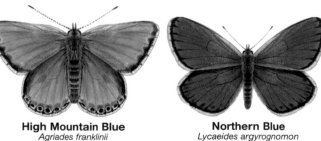

High Mountain Blue
Agriades franklinii
To 1 in. (3 cm)

Northern Blue
Lycaeides argyrognomon
To 1.25 in. (3.2 cm)

Upperwings   Underwings
Silvery Blue
Glaucopsyche lygdamus
To 1.25 in. (3.2 cm)
Underwings are silvery.

GOSSAMER-WINGED BUTTERFLIES

Upperwings   Underwings
Western Tailed Blue
Cupido amyntula
To 1.25 in. (3.2 cm)
Note orange mark above tail on hindwings.

Spring Azure
Celastrina ladon
To 1.25 in. (3.2 cm)
One of the earliest spring butterflies.

American Copper
Lycaena phlaeas
To 1.25 in. (3.2 cm)
Common in disturbed areas and along roadsides.

Mariposa Copper
Lycaena mariposa
To 1 in. (3 cm)

Dorcas Copper
Lycaena dorcas
To 1 in. (3 cm)
Copper wings have deep purplish spots.

Hoary Elfin
Incisalia polios
To 1 in. (3 cm)
Wing margins are silvery.

Brown Elfin
Incisalia augustinus
To 1 in. (3 cm)

BRUSHFOOTS

This family is named for its small forelegs that they use to "taste" food.

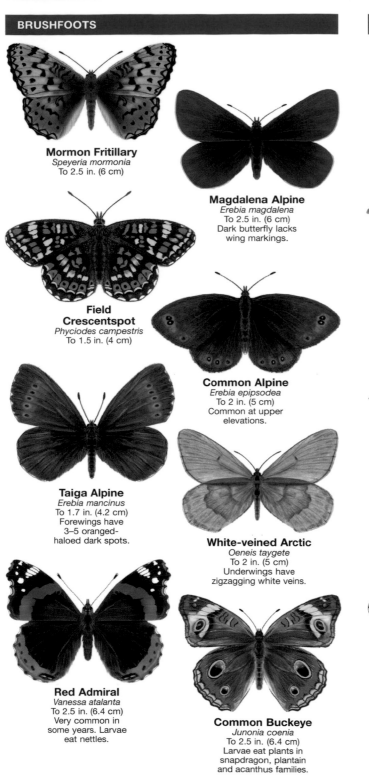

White Admiral
Limenitis arthemis
To 3 in. (8 cm)
Common in upland deciduous forests.

Compton Tortoiseshell
Nymphalis vaualbum
To 3 in. (8 cm)

Milbert's Tortoiseshell
Aglais milberti
To 2 in. (5 cm)

Napaea Fritillary
Boloria napaea
To 2 in. (5 cm)

Silver-bordered Fritillary
Boloria selene
To 2 in. (5 cm)
Underwings feature rows of metallic silver spots.

Polaris Fritillary
Boloria polaris
To 1.5 in. (4 cm)

Freya's Fritillary
Boloria freija
To 1.7 in. (4.2 cm)

Arctic Fritillary
Boloria chariclea
To 1.5 in. (4 cm)

BRUSHFOOTS

Mormon Fritillary
Speyeria mormonia
To 2.5 in. (6 cm)

Magdalena Alpine
Erebia magdalena
To 2 in. (5 cm)
Dark butterfly lacks wing markings.

Field Crescentspot
Phyciodes campestris
To 1.5 in. (4 cm)

Common Alpine
Erebia epipsodea
To 2 in. (5 cm)
Common at upper elevations.

Taiga Alpine
Erebia mancinus
To 1.7 in. (4.2 cm)
Forewings have 3–5 orange-haloed dark spots.

White-veined Arctic
Oeneis taygete
To 2 in. (5 cm)
Underwings have zigzagging white veins.

Red Admiral
Vanessa atalanta
To 2.5 in. (6.4 cm)
Very common in some years. Larvae eat nettles.

Common Buckeye
Junonia coenia
To 2.5 in. (6.4 cm)
Larvae eat plants in snapdragon, plantain and acanthus families.

BRUSHFOOTS

Polixenes Arctic
Oeneis polixenes
To 1.75 in. (4.5 cm)

Jutta Arctic
Oenis jutta
To 2 in. (5 cm)

Green Comma
Polygonia faunus
To 2 in. (5 cm)
Note ragged wing margins and yellowish spotting.

Hoary Comma
Polygonia gracilis
To 1.5 in. (4 cm)

Mourning Cloak
Nymphalis antiopa
To 3.5 in. (9 cm)
Emerges during the first spring thaw. Found in a variety of habitats.

Kodiak Ringlet
Coenonympha kodiak
To 1.5 in. (4 cm)

Upperwings

Painted Lady
Vanessa cardui
To 2.5 in. (6 cm)
Tip of forewing is dark with white spots.

Underwings

MOTHS

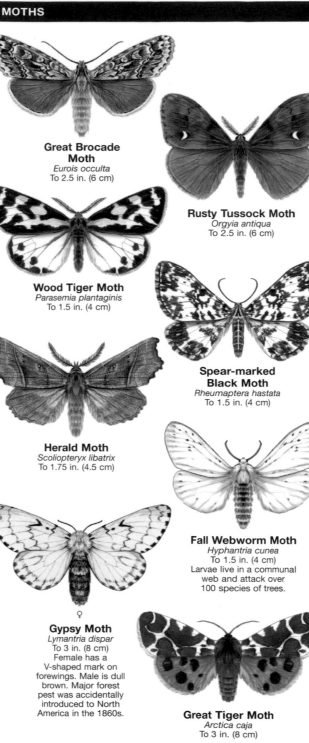

Great Brocade Moth
Euroris occulta
To 2.5 in. (6 cm)

Rusty Tussock Moth
Orgyia antiqua
To 2.5 in. (6 cm)

Wood Tiger Moth
Parasemia plantaginis
To 1.5 in. (4 cm)

Spear-marked Black Moth
Rheumaptera hastata
To 1.5 in. (4 cm)

Herald Moth
Scoliopteryx libatrix
To 1.75 in. (4.5 cm)

Fall Webworm Moth
Hyphantria cunea
To 1.5 in. (4 cm)
Larvae live in a communal web and attack over 100 species of trees.

♀
Gypsy Moth
Lymantria dispar
To 3 in. (8 cm)
Female has a V-shaped mark on forewings. Male is dull brown. Major forest pest was accidentally introduced to North America in the 1860s.

Great Tiger Moth
Arctica caja
To 3 in. (8 cm)

OTHER POLLINATORS

About 75% of the crop plants grown worldwide depend on pollinators – bees, butterflies, birds, bats and other animals – for fertilization and reproduction. Although some species of plants are pollinated by the wind and water, the vast majority (almost 90%) need the help of animals to act as pollinating agents. More than 1,000 of the world's most important foods, beverages and medicines are derived from plants that require pollination by animals.

Pollinating animals worldwide are threatened due to loss of habitat, introduced and invasive species, pesticides, diseases and parasites.

Bees, Wasps & Flies

North America is home to approximately 4,000 species of bees. Of these, the most important crop pollinators are wild native honey bees and managed colonies of European honey bees. Other important flying insects include bumble bees, mason bees, carpenter bees, wasps and numerous flies. With honey bee populations in huge decline due to certain illnesses and habitat loss, this can have a huge impact on food production in North America.

HONEY BEE ANATOMY

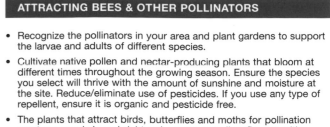

Beetles

The living jewels of the bug world, beetles are the dominant life group on the earth with about 400,000 species found in all habitats except the polar regions and the oceans. They are invaluable to ecosystems as both pollinators and scavengers, feeding on dead animals and fallen trees to recycle nutrients back into the soil. Some, however, are serious pests and cause great harm to living plants (trees, crops). Learn to recognize the good from the bad and involve your local land management and pest control resources to mitigate the spread of harmful beetles.

BEETLE ANATOMY

Birds, Bats & Other Animals

More than 50 species of North American birds occasionally feed on plant nectar and blossoms, but it is the primary food source for hummingbirds and orioles. Sugar water feeders are a good way to supplement the energy of nectar drinkers, but it is far better to plant flowers and shrubs that provide native sources of nutrient-rich nectar. While very common in tropical climates around the world, only three species of nectar-feeding bats are found in the southwestern U.S. They are important pollinators of desert plants including large cacti (organ pipe, saguaro), agaves and century plants. Rodents, lizards and small mammals like mice also pollinate plants when feeding on their nectar and flower heads.

Rufous Hummingbird

Long-nosed Bat

ATTRACTING BEES & OTHER POLLINATORS

- Recognize the pollinators in your area and plant gardens to support the larvae and adults of different species.
- Cultivate native pollen and nectar-producing plants that bloom at different times throughout the growing season. Ensure the species you select will thrive with the amount of sunshine and moisture at the site. Reduce/eliminate use of pesticides. If you use any type of repellent, ensure it is organic and pesticide free.
- The plants that attract birds, butterflies and moths for pollination most commonly have bright red, orange or yellow flowers with very little scent. Butterflies prefer flat-topped "cluster" flowers. Hummingbirds prefer tube or funnel-shaped flowers.
- Create areas, out of the sun, where pollinators can rest and avoid predation while foraging.
- Supply water for both drinking and bathing. Create shallow puddles for bees and butterflies.
- Create nesting boxes or brushy areas that provide protection from predation and are suitable for pollinators to raise their young.
- Learn to recognize the good and bad garden bugs.

CATERPILLARS

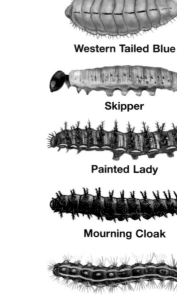

Western Tailed Blue

Cabbage White

Skipper

Alpine

Painted Lady

Common Sulphur

Mourning Cloak

Red Admiral

Gypsy Moth

Rusty Tussock Moth

Fall Webworm Moth

Webworm Web